You Are My Sun and I Am Your Luna

BY LISA HURD

WestBow Press books may be ordered through booksellers or by contacting:

WestBow Press
A Division of Thomas Nelson & Zondervan
1663 Liberty Drive
Bloomington, IN 47403
www.westbowpress.com
844-714-3454

ISBN: 978-1-6642-8726-6 (sc)
ISBN: 978-1-6642-8727-3 (hc)
ISBN: 978-1-6642-8725-9 (e)

Library of Congress Control Number: 2022923507

Print information available on the last page.

WestBow Press rev. date: 12/16/2022

WESTBOW
PRESS®
A DIVISION OF THOMAS NELSON
& ZONDERVAN

You are my Sun.

My seed was planted and you kept me
safe as I grew and grew, nourishing
the life that was forming inside you.

I am your Luna.

At night, you dreamt of me, what I
would look like, how special I would be.

You are my Sun.

The warmth of your voice kept me happy
and healthy. The warmth of your touch
let me know you would always be there.

I am your Luna.

As I got bigger, you felt me move and my body danced across your skin. I would come awake at night just as you were getting ready for sleep.

You are my Sun.

You were the first person I could see,
feel, touch and smell when I came into
the world. You brought me close with
your loving arms and didn't let go.

I am your Luna.

At night I kept you up, although you were tired, you took me into your arms and brought me comfort and peace.

You are my Sun.

You provide me with all that I need to grow and thrive; I get bigger every day.

I am your Luna.

Each night you help me relax, to fall
asleep so my dreams can be sweet.

You are my Sun.

Every morning I look at you and smile. We have our cuddle time, we document the day with pictures, you teach me all you know.

I am your Luna.

I don't want our day to end.

You are my Sun.

You are my everything, my light in this world and you make me happy, Mommy. Even if you have been sad, your love shines through.

....My love for you is as big as the Moon and I will always be your light in the dark because **I am your Luna**... my brightness comes from **my Sun**.

Printed in the United States
by Baker & Taylor Publisher Services